I0087983

Praise for *My Father's Speech*

"*My Father's Speech* is a fascinating window into the world of growing up in coal country. There's not enough poetry, or writing in general, that explores the work-a-day world and the lives of 'ordinary' people. Katherine Cottle has given us an excellent example of what a good writer can do with such rich source material."
—Reginald Harris
Judge and Poet, *Ten Tongues*
Finalist, Lambda Literary Award

"Katherine Cottle's poems take risks, and spend time diving under the surface of questions about self, history, family, and religion. They took me into a world I knew nothing about, but found fascinating."
—Christine Stewart
Judge and Director, "Write Here, Write Now" Workshops
MFA in Creative Writing (Poetry), University of Maryland

My Father's Speech

My Father's Speech

Poems by Katherine Cottle

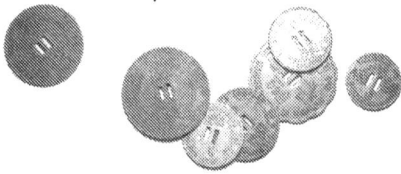

Apprentice House
Baltimore, Maryland
www.apprenticehouse.com

© 2008, Katherine Cottle

Grateful acknowledgment is made to the editors of the following journals and anthology for publishing versions of the following poems:

Eclipse: "Digging to China"
The Maryland Poetry Review: "Two Bats"
The Mochila Review: "Grace"
The New Laurel Review: "Burying the Cat"
Ravishing DisUnities: Real Ghazals in English: "Consider"
River Oak Review: "Day Force, Cranberry Mine, West Virginia, 1956"
Rockhurst Review: "What I Don't Talk About"
Silk Road: "Appalachian Portraits"
SLANT: "My Father's Speech"
Willow Springs: "Coleslaw"

ISBN: 978-1-934074-30-5

All rights reserved. No part of this book may be reproduced or transmitted in any form or by any means, electronic or mechanical, including photocopy, recording, or any information storage and retrieval system, without prior permission from the publisher (except by reviewers who may quote brief passages).

Printed in the United States of America

First Edition
10 9 8 7 6 5 4 3 2 1

Cover photo: Elizabeth Watson
Cover art and design: Elizabeth Watson
Internal design: Regina Lyons

Published by Apprentice House
The Future of Publishing…Today!

Apprentice House
Communication Department
Loyola College in Maryland
4501 N. Charles Street
Baltimore, MD 21210

410.617.5265 • 410.617.5040 (fax)
www.ApprenticeHouse.com • info@ApprenticeHouse.com

For my story-tellers: my father, Harvey Cottle, and his parents, Robert and Elizabeth Cottle.

On the cover: West Virginia Coal Scrip

Coal mining began on a large scale in West Virginia in the late 19th century. Due to the rugged terrain and the distance from banks, the larger mining companies issued token money to pay their miners. By the 1920s the use of coal mine scrip had become common practice. Scrip was part of a very profitable system that the companies used to increase the profits on their operations.

This is how it worked. The scrip was issued as an advance against wages. It was good only at the company store. The rices were high and there was no competition. The miner would receive U.S. currency on payday only if he did not owe the company money. In addition to groceries, clothing, and other necessities for the home, a miner had to pay rent to live in a company house, pay for his own tools, powder, caps, ther mining supplies, pay doctor bills (company doctor), water (company wells), electricity (company power plant), blacksmithing charges on his tools (company blacksmith), and contribute to a compulsory funeral fund. The charges were endless and take home pay scarce.

The companies first used books of paper coupons and then issued tokens. They were made from aluminum, copper, brass, paper fiber, bronze, nickel, wood, and zinc. Most metal tokens were punched with the initial letter of the town in which it was used. The punch-out made it easier to recognize and sort the tokens. Scrip is now a thing of the past. The company towns and the company stores are fading fast. Most are gone. The scrip remains to tell the story.

The scrip that appears on this chapbook's cover was provided by Robert Cottle, the poet's grandfather.

Table of Contents

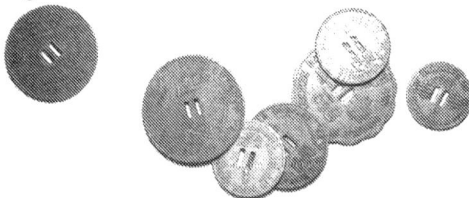

My F a t h e r ' s   S p e e c h

It isn't a twang that escapes
from your voice when Uncle Charlie calls,
but a deeper country that surfaces
when you think no one is listening.

If I could pull it from your mouth
it would be black as coal dust,
the tiny grains of rock that climbed
through the miners' lungs,
leaving your father's chest a wilt
of ragged breath.

If I could taste it, it would be
grits and coleslaw, greasy gravy
over biscuits and egg.

But you keep the edge hidden well,
tucked behind a white button down and tie,
your body aging as quickly as a young boy's.

It is hard to believe that it is the same body
as the one in the picture I dig out
from beneath your dresser each Christmas--
the class picture, the one without
your front tooth.

The boy there is smiling,
words about to escape from his mouth.
The accent does not matter.
All he knows is what he has known:

That he is a boy,
that the ground becomes cool each evening,
that his father comes home after dinner
from the day shift,
that the mountain with the tallest pines
is the last point the sun will hit
before his mother will call him
into the house for the night.

Coal Camp
    Cranberry Mine
        West Virginia, 1950

It is a picture of a picture, an old photograph
tacked down, then focused and snapped
on a crumbling plank of wood.

In it, my grandmother squats above the ground,
her stiff house dress folding in sharp corners
underneath her locked knees.

She is holding my father in her right arm.
He is such a big baby
that soon she will need a better grip.

Peeking out from beneath her left arm,
my aunt's eyes squint into tears
while her forefinger hooks down from her mouth.

My aunt's light hair still looks as soft as feathers,
too slippery to braid into the plaits
my grandmother will someday weave for her.

My grandmother's coarse dark hair is pulled back,
away from her children's reach, showing strong cheeks
already darkening the way my father's eventually will.

But here, tight in her young arm,
my father's cheeks are still pale.
Here, he opens his eyes in wonder.

Behind them, a shed's phantom legs fade
before touching the ground,
while a wire fence blends into the shadow of the mountain.

The background is uncertain, almost not there,
yet my grandmother is certain,
her work dress crackling in spite of the dust.

She defies it all: the black and white photo,
the double distance of the frame,
the spotted lens pulling her further and further away.

She lets it be known that she will always be here,
this stubborn eighteen year old, always she will hold
her children like this--close by, a little frightened.
She will ignore the shaking muscles in her calves
while her children are still growing,
until, when she no longer needs to hold their weight,

she will fall, face first,
her dress finally releasing from its form,
then spreading out into wings.

D a y   F o r c e
  C r a n b e r r y   M i n e
    W e s t   V i r g i n i a ,   1 9 5 6

    There you are. Fifth one from the right. A man so thin and young, the only way I recognize you is the nose-- the long pointed nose that hints a line, an uncooperative slope against the three horizontal rows of positioned miners. It is almost like a school picture, lined up by height, the shortest made to grip their knees to the ground. You were tall then, in the back row, your arms relaxed in the moment of something different, something other than the ten hours underground, blasting the seams, then shoveling, dust climbing day by day into your lungs. The other men look less comfortable, perhaps knowing they will not get out, the way you now remember the two in the front right will be crushed the next week, only their arms left whole after the unexpected fall of rock. Perhaps they know it will be another twenty years before you leave, that the coal will also find a way through your skin, black scars running over your body like maps. All of the men's eyes are open, even yours. Perhaps it is the flash, the pinching yellow so much like the sun, that holds them there. Perhaps, like the carbide glow from your helmet, the light meant safety, someone to watch your back, that you were not the only one down there.

Appalachian Portraits
(After Photographs by Shelby Lee Adams)

I.

The Hog Killing
Beehive, Kentucky
1990

At first, the teats look like shoelace holes,
two tracks running symmetrically
down either side of the hanging carcass,
the body carved straight down the middle
from hip to head.
Only the head is missing,
placed snout-up in a metal pail.
The organs already removed,
the back ribcage peeks through,
exposed and dark like a hidden closet.

The Napier family smiles as the blood
drips onto the dirt.
John, the father, sits on a stool,
the ax resting in his thick hands,
while his wife, Berthie,
creeps closer to the camera,
a rusty knife clutched in her left hand.
Behind them, their four boys
smirk behind cowboy hats,
cigarettes dangling
out of the corners of their mouths.

The sons stand on either side
of the rotting wood brace,
framing the tacked up hog,
its legs stretched across the top,
pulled apart far enough
to open the pelvis even more,
to let the blood finish draining.

The boys' smiles are suspicious,
like they are holding something back.
Their mouths tightly closed,
they look as if they will burst with their secret.
But, for now, they are silent,
eyes focused on the photographer,
the Kentucky dusk creeping in,
just about to cover them.

II.

Holiness Boy with Serpent
Box and Poison Jar
Harlan County, 1987

This could be any boy,
out in front of a church,
baseball cap pulled down low,
almost covering his eyes,
skin pale and clean
from a morning washing.

This could be any boy,
paused for a picture after service,
already itching
to head to the creek for a swim.
Even the black tennis shoes
underneath the dress pants
spell movement,
the laces double knotted
in preparation of action,
his black baseball cap
fitted tight with its big white decals:
Jesus is my God.

This could be any nephew,
brother, or cousin,
bracing the serpent box
with his right hand,
the snake moving strong and dark
behind the two windows
of the cherry case,
his hand clasping the golden handle,
the hinges freshly polished and gleaming
like a new coffin.

This could be any Boy Scout,
neighbor, or student,
raising the poison jar
with his other hand,
presenting his latest show-and-tell,
the mason jar half full
of clear liquid,
almost as simple as water.
Only, his careful grip admits
it is more,
that the jar is something special,
that the holiness followers
will soon drink
to show their faith.

This could be any child,
and here,
he is still unnamed.
Holiness boy, child of God.
His face unbending,
already stubborn
in its eight year old presence,
already a follower,
one of the faithful,
a believer.

III.
 Bert Holding Homemade
     Jew's Harp
          Knott County,
             Kentucky, 1987

The way he is holding
the homemade Jew's harp,
carefully crafted from a rusty bed spring
and a Prince Albert tobacco can,
makes everything else
in the picture insignificant:
his filthy button down shirt,
uneven pants, wrinkled chin,
his crooked body leaning
between an old tire and a rusting stove.
The trees even back away
from the instrument,
cradled in his hands like a newborn,
and the music that only he can hear
since his sunstroke thirty years ago:

the swipe of his grandmother's hand
across his four year old forehead,
the sound of the river
on the top of Sloan mountain,
the voice that tells him
to walk twenty miles everyday,
only stopping
when his body gives out,
when all he can hear is the breath
of God just behind his dirty ears.

I V .

Lee Hall, Retired Coal Miner,
Camp Branch, 1 9 8 3

He is dressed formally,
a dark oxford buttoned
to the neck,
a stiff conductor's cap
centered above his ears.
Both fabrics cover
all traces of his head and body,
leaving only his face
as the marker,
as the stone.

His mouth, caved in
from the lack of teeth,
puckers behind prickly stubble.
His left eye,
his only eye,
looks straight on
at the camera,
stern amid the landscape
of wrinkles and scars
carved deep into his face.

At first, it looks as if
he is squinting,
the sun too bright
on this Tuesday.
Or, perhaps,
the painful pop
of the camera flash has
caused his right eye
to sink back, to hide
in the soft bed of skin that,
looking closer,
is his only guard
against a shadowed hole,
against an empty socket
that only mimics sight.

V.

Harlan and Cathy with
Water Pump
Cannie Creek, 1992

Harlan is the one
with his hand on the water pump.
His wife, Cathy,
is three steps behind
in the doorway of the house.

The pump is almost as tall
as Harlan is,
mainly because of his slump,
his back curled over
like a knotted tree.
And he is barely any wider
than the arm
of the rusting metal pump,
his skeletal frame
hidden behind a long sleeved
cowboy shirt,
tucked into his clean white pants.
The bones are sharpest
at his face,
his nose and cheekbones
jutting out,
his dark eyes sunken in,
and without any make-up,
he could easily walk onto
the set of a Boris Karloff film,
his black hair over-parted
and greased above his right ear.

Back in the doorway,
in the opening to the kitchen,
Cathy holds the butter churn
with her chubby hand,
her huge body filling
the entire doorway.
She matches her husband
with her white pants and dark shirt.
Only, her pants are four times
the size of her husband's,
her belly pushing hard
against the seams,
and her shirt is more faded,
with a "Kentucky" decal
stretched across her lumpy breasts.
Her face, although layered
with extra folds,
holds the same paleness,
the same sunken eyes,
the same unwashed and limp hair.

The difference between them
is merely their ingredients--
his body is a creek,
clear with water,
his hands blue and shaking
from its cold;
her body is solid,
layered with the land,
taking in everything
that she can claim as her own.

Together,
their days continue this way,
with and without,
the water pumping,
the butter churning.

S p i t   C a n

The golden letters were faded in spots,
eaten from rust, while a grey film covered
Maxwell House with wet webbing.
Underneath the peeling blue paint,
the metal had broken through,
making it look like a mechanic's tool,
an invention to improve an invention.
Or, it could have been an old sea relic,
flakes falling from the side with each touch.

I imagined a sound would echo when putting
it to the ear: drip of soggy swamp,
suck of a tennis shoe through the mud.
But inside, in a hidden world of juice and mucus,
my grandfather's chewing tobacco spit
settled in a tiny pool of sewage.
Underneath the moldy top layer,
leaves and strings clung to the ribbed walls
the way moss clung to the banks of our creek.

What it was like in there was so adult
that I wanted it—the stench,
the chunks, the look of age and time.
I spit my milk into a Folger's can,
then stirred in dirt and grass
until even a stick could not break
the thick heart of my creation.

A r r o w h e a d

The chiggers broke out three days
after we returned.
My father lay in bed,
bumps erupting over his body
in rows of little hills.
It was all he could do
not to itch them,
his arms pressed hard
against the sheets
in mouth clenching restraint.

On the dresser, his discovery:
a sulfur yellow arrowhead,
dug up from his uncle's backyard.
He spent the rest of the vacation
digging for more.
Shoveling through the dirt,
he hauled away the layered years,
examining every splinter,
every bit of hard rock.

Later, his body
a vessel of scampering life,
he examined the arrowhead—
his prized trophy, his war medal.
He rubbed his scabbed fingers
over the sharp, carved edges,
imagining the battle,
the sharp piercing of the prey.

Even now, in bed,
when the house's sounds
are buried under the weight of night,
he dreams of the tool,
sharpening stone heavy
in his other hand,
and wakes to the grind of stone
against stone, the cry of his own
palms—silent, bleeding, alone.

Tattoos

I.

The wrinkled black lines stretch
across my grandfather's legs,
constant reminders of the mines,
of a life under, not above,
in a world hidden in the dark.
It is coal dust still trapped inside,
grainy insects forever caught
in the scars of his old healed cuts.
They twist and turn like mountain roads,
hunting for a destination,
for a final resting place.

II.

My father's initials peek out
from beneath his undershirt sleeve.
Around the letters,
dotted black arrows frame his name
like a rusty weathervane,
pointing North, South, East, and West—
It is an early compass of his future,
the permanent signature
of his fifteen year old cousin's shaky hand.

III.

The light black edges of the sword
on my husband's shoulder are starting to fade.
No longer sharp, they look more like veins
than honor or protection.
Defining skin, rather than battle,
they arm him with the illusion
of strength, of marked force,
as he chooses *fight*
time and time again
over *flee*.

C o l e s l a w

I.

Just to taste.
Slice the cabbage thin, you said.
No recipe, no need.
The vinegar, mayonnaise,
and sprinkles of sugar
formed sweet crusts.
Keep adding to taste, you said.
I remember your hands,
such strong meaty hands—
the sugar seemed to melt
right into them.
We sat in the kitchen, stirred,
and licked our fingers.
The slaw tasted sweet
as ice cream.

II.

I was twelve when
we entered the pawn shop.
Old Jack, this is my
granddaughter, you said.
She fights the boys off
just like I did.
We walked out with
a tiny engagement ring,
so small it barely fit my pinky.
Old Jack winked when we left,
a $75 I.O.U. slipped
under the adding machine.
You'll never see sixteen again,

that's what they told me
at your age, you said.
You're just like me.
You just keep fightin'
them boys off.

III.

Today, as I stop by the hospital
this Thanksgiving,
I hear you have finished another quilt.
I wish I had a basket of food to bring,
some small cornucopia,
so that we could spread the quilt
out over the cold floor
and ring the nurses to join us in thanks,
while I set out the hot turkey slices,
cranberries, pumpkin pie,
and the coleslaw
I have so often tried to copy.
It does not taste like yours.
There is always too much mayonnaise
or too much vinegar,
and I can never find the right taste
between the sweet
and the sour.

Grace

"*And these signs shall follow them that believe; in My name shall they cast out devils; they shall take up serpents; and if they drink any deadly thing, it shall not hurt them; they shall lay hands on the sick, and they shall recover.*"
—Mark 16: 17-18

I.

Grace:
a girl's name,
the sound of light wind
against a window.
Grace of God:
those chosen before,
the ones who will
live with God after death.
And me:
next to my grandmother
on the wood pew,
wondering where the sign
could be, the mark
to let me know
I was chosen.
Maybe it was on the inside,
but I was too scared
to go into the outhouse,
too scared to venture
past the rotten planks
and spider webs,
to pull up my dress and look.
I sat through the sermons,
tracing each organ
with my mind,
turning the heart's folds over
to look along the seams,

pushing each sponge of lung in
until there was a mark,
a dark shadow, some sign to show
I would never end.

II.

I have to take my father's word—
that they spoke in tongues,
that they rolled on the floor
as if in pain.

I was not there,
in the mountains of West Virginia.
I was born later,
in a city where tongues

are written down.
I can only imagine:
a woman falling to the dirt floor,
a man opening his mouth

wide enough for eight syllable
words to slither out.
Kids, too, whispering
under their breath.

It is the church no one
will ever find
on any map or trail.
But my father swears

it is still there,
its members chanting and dancing,
the way they continue to speak
to him through his dreams.

Only, in his dreams, he can
finally translate their words:

We see you, little boy,
watching us through the window.

Come in, meet the almighty Lord.
Feel what it is you will
spend the rest of your life
trying to explain.

III.

Holiness.
His holiness.
Anoint me, oh Lord.

I believe.
I will take the serpent in my hands.
See how I hold its head

and it does not bite.
See my faith.
Its rattle shakes

like a can of dried beans.
Its head swings back and forth
below my wrist.

The pattern of its body
is like the bottom of the river.
I will not feel the tight grip

around my arm.
You are here.
In me.

I will close my eyes.
Your work. Your spirit.
The serpent will have no power.

Its fangs on my hand are nothing.
I am a Holiness child.

I am your child.
Lord, soothe the serpent.
I am numb. I am cold.
Oh Lord,

your power will overcome.
Your sweet ways will anoint.
I believe.

IV.

. . . and she was but a child,
Brothers and Sisters, and a child
under twelve is already
in God's hands, already
a chosen one. Do not
worry, Brothers and Sisters,
the Red Devil lye did not kill her,
oh no, because she was one of God's
already, and the strychnine
did not kill her. No, it was God's
will. Take the jar in your hands,
Brothers and Sisters. Show God
we still believe. Drink for God.
God, we will not leave you. . .

V.

She is becoming violent,
the doctor tells us,
and we nod,
knowing full well she has already
been this way for weeks,
that this is only the first time
he has seen it.

They become children again:
diapers, feeding,
everything centered around themselves.

The mind turns back,
caught in the rusted groove
between third grade
and a jealous sister.

But the woman here does not even know
we are talking about her.
Packed tight under the covers,
she scrapes her nail
across the seams of the top quilt.

I could stick this nail
right through your eye,
she tells me.
Don't tell me what to do!
There have already been
too many close calls.
She wants to hurt someone,
anyone, anything
to stop what she has
forgotten is happening.

*

Where are my boys?
Where is somebody to take care of me?

The oxygen tube coils around
her head like a tired serpent.

The nurses' hands stick patches of poison
onto her heart.

We pour 25 more pills
into her throat.

*

Each night, her dead husband enters her dreams
and she moves closer to a place without words,
to a God she has never doubted.
She does not need a sign.
Unlike me, she is tired of trying.
Unlike me, she is not worried if she will rise up—
in life, after death.

Take my bible, she says.
I have marked the places.

Her hands shake over the passages.
She pretends to read-- she must imagine
the story to the words she can no longer see,
the way I once imagined
the holiness people in her stories.
And, like a child, it is not the language
that she remembers, but the image,
the sign, the comfort in tracing
what has come before and what will
faithfully follow.

Two Bats

This morning, walking back from the mailbox,
I saw their tight bodies, two purple bruises,
wrinkled fists of limp skin and hair
left in knots on top of the driveway.

Was it bad direction that caused a low angle?
Or the slight shadow of concrete
so close to the plane of night?
Their symmetry shines like a child's closed lids.

And together, they must have fallen, or hit,
causing a split second of whisper and bump,
a landing like hard rain, the body a warm drop.

Unlike them, did you doubt the moment before?
Or did you believe the ground would save you
when the sky could not?

Burying the Cat

If I could remember
where the others were planted—
I would know this spot was right,
that the shovel would hit
bone or the dull crinkle
of an old grocery bag—
and that would be something,
if not the only thing,
to say this is the place.

But there is no sign
as I slice into clay,
chipped rock, ripping
through weed and wet clover.

This shoebox under my arm
could be any shoe,
plant, or child.
Patting the dirt overtop
is as simple as plucking
a blade of grass.

This stick I wedge down
will be gone the next time,
though I swear I will remember,
the way an urgent name
or number is always
the first thing to go.

Consider
        (a ghazal)

A child stares at the wall for hours,
understanding Creation in less than 4 hours.

A dog twitches, calm quiver from sleep,
as dawn approaches, signaling more hours.

Sand crabs dig to escape from the water.
The tide follows neither rules nor hours.

Are considerations too slippery to see?
Is there ever anything but pain or hours?

The thick swell of a tongue rolls back.
What is left to consider? These are war hours.

Katherine means "pure," as in "God" or "girl";
I do not recognize my own name or face for hours

What I Don't Talk About

is my great uncle
and the two shots into
his own brother's chest,
the way his brother's mouth
puckered just like their father's
before dying,
and the next six years in prison,
waiting for cancer
to slowly finish the revenge.

What I intentionally leave out
is my great grandfather,
the rumors of white sheets
and missing nights,
of bloody pants
and an early death
in the hills of West Virginia.

But the person who unnerves me
the most is the poet—
her fear of the truth,
and her need to open
only the good quiet sores
onto the page.

What I don't tell people
is her own secrets—
her need to love more people
than there is room for,
to let difference take her life
down a path she would
never expect.

Digging to China

Some children believe it can happen.
Shovel in hand,
they dig until their fingers
break into blisters.
It's a deep hole,
but a day is equal to a year
for a child,
a hole to China is as possible
as a hole in the fence.

I always knew it would be
impossible to get there.
Not because of its distance,
but because of the tool.
I knew I would have to fly—
on a bird's wing, a cloud,
or the knotted string
of my birthday balloons.

*

At night, I dreamt of the others' attempts:
a small boy's hand,
exhausted from years of digging,
falling limp like a dead turtle head.
How far did he make it?
Through eight layers of rock?
Past a lost stream and a cave of tar?
I pictured transparent creatures breaking
through the walls of his tunnel,
staring at him with their white gauzy eyes.

When it became so hot that he thought
his body would burst,
did he know to angle his dig,

to tunnel around the fiery center,
just missing the core of lava,
the cry of a liquid that has only dreamt
of touching human skin?

It must be lonely inside the earth.
Perhaps the boy pretended
to be holding his best friend's hand
when a snake slithered across his foot.
Or, perhaps he felt cozy,
being that tight inside,
knowing there was no more space left,
not even enough room to squeeze in
another limb.

*

I pretzeled myself
into the basement window well
most afternoons.
I named all of the rocks
and knew every scratch
on the rusting metal frame,
even the temperature of the ground
around the base of my finger.
Sometimes, I pushed my finger
into the earth for the coolness,
but mostly, it was the texture,
the dry dust under my nail that I liked,
the hard grip against my joints.
And when I pulled it out,
there was always a pattern,
a temporary map on my skin.

*

In the best dreams,
I could make it to the other side,
through the grime and grit,

my shovel becoming a hybrid
of a hollowed pole and a Slurpee straw.
The shovel would grow
the entire diameter of the earth,
digging down like a mine
or the pump of a new well.
I would slide through,
uncut and dazed,
like I was on a waterslide
in an amusement park.
And, like most dreams,
China would become my own,
the language a sweet mouthful
of sesame and dry leaf.
The people were friends that I
had somehow forgotten
I hadn't visited in years.
My room would wait, clean and neat,
kept by a Chinese mother
who hung my first grade
handwriting award in a gold frame
above my dresser.

*

The teacher pulled the world map
down in front of the chalkboard.
No, it doesn't look like that,
I told her.
*China isn't red. It isn't shaped
like a melting peanut.
My China is cold, the color blue,
with crystal streets,
and mountains that drift
back and forth from its shore.
My China is the smell of warm
porcelain, the feel of a spoon
against the palm.*
This is China, she said,
The map says so.

*

We are studying geometry
and I am placing the tip of the compass
on Maryland, trying to measure
the distance to China.
The globe is dusty and my compass
keeps slipping.
When I jab the blunt tip through Baltimore,
the leg slides through,
and I feel the emptiness inside.
The space under the world
is a vacuum, silent and unmoving.
If I pull the leg of the compass out,
all of the breath will be released,
and I fear the world won't be able
to contain itself.
The air that passes through
will not know the difference
between the ridged mountains
and the cardboard lining.

*

In the folktale,
the Emperor's beautiful daughter
lives in the clouds
with an invisible staircase
as her only passage to earth.
Because of the invisible staircase,
the suitors cannot reach her.
Only the one who closes his eyes
feels the entrance,
the sharp corner of the first step
against his shin.
The tale ends there, with him climbing,
eyes still closed,
hands feeling for the next step.

*

The shadow of a maple leaf
moves across my arm as I write.
I feel its weight heavier
than any real leaf.
In the shadow, its veins are undefined,
and I have to imagine the roundness
of the stem, the tears
along the jagged edges.
Beneath my bare feet,
the sharp ridges of uncut grass
grow in a way that can only be seen
with my eyes closed.
The angles of their lives reach
far beyond my telling.
Above, on the telephone line,
a robin readies for flight.
While I scratch out and re-write,
hunting for preciseness,
she lifts,
not calculating the distance
or the exact measurement of her journey,
only the ability of the wind
to keep her up,
the sound of the other birds up ahead,
calling, directing her motion.
China, I hear them sing
in their high range of pinched voice.
Underneath, the world sighs,
opens a small pore,
and for a moment I fit through,
just barely.

Poet's Note

My Father's Speech evolved from poems written over a span
of seventeen years. Initially, I viewed the poems as individual
pieces, but eventually I realized that they all came from the
same source in my mind, a shaft which held the stories of
my father, his parents, and an almost forgotten world of coal
mining and poverty. Uncovering this history enabled me to
bring my lineage to the surface and allowed me to find my own
hidden speech, buried within the layers of words.

About the Poet

Katherine Cottle received her BA from Goucher College and
her MFA from the University of Maryland at College Park.
Her work has appeared in such literary journals as *Eclipse,*
The Greensboro Review, Karamu, The Mochila Review, The
New Delta Review, Poetry East, and *River Oak Review,* as well
as in several national anthologies. She is currently a distance
education instructor through Johns Hopkins University's
Center for Talented Youth writing program. She lives in Glen
Arm, Maryland, with her husband and children, Addison and
Ellie.

Apprentice House
Annual Chapbook Competition
Submission Guidelines

Apprentice House is the country's only campus-based, student-staffed book publisher. Directed by professors and industry professionals, it is a nonprofit activity of the Communication Department at Loyola College in Maryland. The Apprentice House model creates an unprecedented collaborative environment among faculty and students.

Apprentice House: the future of publishing...today!

The poetry chapbook contest is for poets previously unpublished in book form. Winner receives $250 prize and 20 copies. There is a $20 submission fee payable to Apprentice House. The annual deadline is April 1 postmark. Submit at least thirty pages of typed poetry manuscript. Mail to: Chapbook Contest, Apprentice House, c/o Communication Department, Loyola College, 4501 N. Charles St., Baltimore, MD 21210.

Contact Apprentice House for complete guidelines at info@apprenticehouse.com or 410-617-5265.

Thank you to this year's judges:

Ned Balbo, poet, Apprentice House editorial board member, and Affiliate Associate Professor in the Writing Department at Loyola College.

Reginald Harris, poet, *Ten Tongues*, which was a finalist for the Lambda Literary Award.

Christine Stewart, poet and novelist, and director of the "Write Here, Write Now" Workshops in Baltimore.

apprentice house

The future of publishing...today!

Apprentice House is the country's only campus-based, student-staffed book publishing company. Directed by professors and industry professionals, it is a nonprofit activity of the Communication Department at Loyola College in Maryland.

Using state-of-the-art technology and an experiential learning model of education, Apprentice House publishes books in untraditional ways. This dual responsibility as publishers and educators creates an unprecedented collaborative environment among faculty and students, while teaching tomorrow's editors, designers, and marketers.

Outside of class, progress on book projects is carried forth by the AH Book Publishing Club, a co-curricular campus organization supported by Loyola College's Office of Student Activities.

Student Project Team for *My Father's Speech*
    Elizabeth Watson '08
    Regina Lyons '08

Eclectic and provocative, Apprentice House titles intend to entertain as well as spark dialogue on a variety of topics.

Financial contributions to sustain the press's work are welcomed. Contributions are tax deductible to the fullest extent allowed by the IRS.

To learn more about Apprentice House books or to obtain submission guidelines, please visit www.ApprenticeHouse.com

Apprentice House
Communication Department
Loyola College in Maryland
4501 N. Charles Street
Baltimore, MD 21210
Ph: 410-617-5265 • Fax: 410-617-5040
info@apprenticehouse.com

www.ingramcontent.com/pod-product-compliance
Lightning Source LLC
Chambersburg PA
CBHW071432040426
42445CB00012BA/1351